## THE SEASON OF LENT AND EAST
## THE POWER OF LOVE

Lent and Easter bring to mind many images of faith - ashes, purple vestments, somber music, abstaining from meat, repentance, palms. They also embody treasured images of new life, springtime, end of winter, hope, Easter eggs, tulips, white lilies. These images of Lent and Easter go hand in hand with our daily comings and goings.

The forty days of Lent are the Christian community's annual retreat. In the early Church, Lent was the time before Easter when new candidates for baptism were being taught the essentials of Christian faith. As these catechumens were being prepared, the baptized members joined them with practices that helped them renew their own faith and helped deepen their commitment to Jesus Christ.

Lent and Easter are intimately joined to the Christian journey of growing into the fullness of what it means to be a baptized member of the Body of Christ. We're invited to join in certain spiritual practices to help us strengthen our faith. Prayer, fasting, alms giving, abstaining from meat and other worldly indulgences are activities where we can experience a greater dependence upon God. These practices are not ends in themselves, but seen as a means in helping us draw closer to God.

Our Lenten journey leads us to Easter when we celebrate the Passion, Death and Resurrection of Jesus Christ. The Triduum, the three days - Holy Thursday, Good Friday and Easter - ritualize the heart and soul of our Christian Faith. If one were to choose the most important days to join with other Christians in worship, these days are those that take us to the source and summit of our faith.

After the Easter Triduum, the other half of our journey from ashes to glory extends through the Seven Weeks of Easter, culminating on Pentecost. Mystagogia describes this time during which the early Christian community helped the newly baptized go deeper into the mysteries of faith. While many of us put more emphasis on the Lenten part of the journey, these seven weeks are equally important as they invite us to experience and share in the joyous victory of God's love over death and darkness.

On this yearly journey from Ash Wednesday to Pentecost, God is there to remind us that love always wins.

5

# HOW TO USE THIS PRAYER BOOK

*T*he nineteen prayers in this book are meant to be savored and enjoyed with no sense of hurry. You'll notice that the early reflections are focused on Lent, followed by those for Holy Week, and finally culminating in the seven weeks of Easter, but you can do them in any order you want. Trust the movement of the Holy Spirit to guide you. Start with one that especially appeals to you and stay with it for as long as it provides grace and inspiration.

Each prayer consists of seven elements:

> a reflection
> a photograph
> a song
> a scripture passage
> a prayer
> a keystone
> a self-examination

Here's a suggestion for how to proceed with each prayer. Begin by listening to the song. Then slowly read the reflection. Then spend some time with the photograph. Don't try to figure it out, but rather let it speak to your heart. After that, read the scripture passage and pay attention to whatever words capture your imagination. Don't rush through it.

As you pray, be mindful of anything that seems to engage your mind and heart. It might be a line from scripture, a lyric from the song, a phrase from the reflection, or some feeling elicited by the photograph. When this happens, it means that there's grace coming to you through that element. Don't be afraid to treasure that moment and stay with it as long as you want. Come back to it later if you are so inspired.

Take a break whenever you need and go about your day. The "keystone" is a simple phrase that anchors the prayer. In practice, the idea is to carry this "keystone" with you outside the times of formal prayer. Repeat it in your heart as you make your way through your daily activities. You might even want to copy it on a piece of paper and place it someplace where you'll be reminded. By recalling the keystone in this way, the prayer becomes even more "centered" in your mind and heart.

Finally, at the end of each day, perhaps as you're crawling into bed to say your nightly prayers, spend a few moments in self-examination, going over your day. The simple questions are provided to help you with this. This part of your prayer is not about counting the ways you've failed, but rather a means of recognizing the moments of grace that have blessed your day.

Spend a week with each of the prayers. Come back to them whenever you have time. Go back to the element that seemed to capture your heart and mind. God's grace can work through any one of them.

# TABLE OF CONTENTS

---

# Ashes
# to
# Ashes

---

*T*he word "Lent" comes from a Germanic term for "springtime," the days when new life emerges from what has lain dormant all winter. It's a most appropriate time for us Christians to make our annual retreat and grow in our relationship with God. By tilling the soil of our faith and nurturing the seeds that have lain fallow in our hearts, God brings new life to birth in us. As we begin our Lenten journey, we are marked on the forehead with a cross, just as we were marked with a cross at our baptism. We are invited to embrace our mortality, for by doing so all the rest of life falls into right perspective. The cross on our forehead is God's promise of new life from the ashes of death.

## SONG

**Ashes to ashes, from dust unto dust,**
**the cross on our forehead, your promise, O God.**
**Ready us to follow the way of your Son,**
**to rise from these ashes, redeemed in the fire of your love.**

Sound the trumpet in Zion; announce from the Lord
that the day of God's favor is ever close at hand.

Rend your hearts not your garments; return to the Lord.
God delights when we offer a truly humble heart.

We have seen in the heavens and held in our hands
what the hand of our Maker can fashion out of dust.

## SCRIPTURE

*S*ee, I have set before you today life and prosperity, death and adversity. If you obey the commandments of the Lord your God that I am commanding you today, by loving the Lord your God, walking in his ways, and observing his commandments, decrees, and ordinances, then you shall live and become numerous, and the Lord your God will bless you in the land that you are entering to possess.

I call heaven and earth to witness against you today that I have set before you life and death, blessings and curses. Choose life so that you and your descendants may live, loving the Lord your God, obeying him, and holding fast to him; for that means life to you and length of days, so that you may live in the land that the Lord swore to give to your ancestors, to Abraham, to Isaac, and to Jacob.

Deuteronomy 30:15-16, 19-20

## PRAYER

Lord and Giver of Life,
in you we live, we move, and have our being.
Nothing - no plant or animal,
no sun or star, no hope or dream -
has its existence outside of you.
On this day most especially,
and during this season of Lent,
help me to be aware of my mortality,
of how precious and fragile life is,
and of how all on this earth will pass away in time.
I pray for this awareness
not so that I feel sad or insignificant,
but that I might keep my eye on the things of God,
and spend my time and energy
on what is most important and of eternal value.
Grant me, O God, the special grace
of seeing all people and things
as you see them.

## KEYSTONE

*"Remember that you are dust."*

## SELF-REFLECTION

- What would I change if I had only a short time to live?
- How can I better attend to what's really important?
- Do I spend my time on things that bring life?

# Let All Who Thirst

*W*ater is such an amazing element, refreshing our parched lips, washing the grime of life from our bodies, soothing our tired bones. But few of us have ever experienced what it's like to be truly thirsty to the point of extreme weakness and dire need. During Lent we are invited to drink deeply of the springs of God's grace, to allow the Word of God to give us new life, to let the rites of Lent refresh our tired souls. God doesn't force us to drink, but the invitation is there if we want it. All we need to do is open ourselves and let God's refreshing grace wash over us. After all, God usually knows what we need better than we do.

# Let All Who Thirst

### SONG

O let all who thirst now come and drink;
come to the living stream.
With your tender hearts and broken dreams,
come to the springs of grace.
Though you have no wealth, no stores of gold,
you can drink to your heart's desire,
till your soul is filled with heaven's joy
here at the font of life.

When you seek my face in light of day,
I will be close at hand.
If you call my name in darkest night,
I will be there to save.
I will keep my promise made of old
to the children of David's line.
I will be your God and you my kin
long as the stars will shine.

As you journey forth to distant lands,
I will protect your way.
I will set my bow among the clouds,
sign of my love and light.
I will bind your heart with righteousness;
I will give you a prophet's tongue.
You shall be for all a sign of hope,
born in the font of grace.

## SCRIPTURE

*T*he people quarreled with Moses, and said, "Give us water to drink." Moses said to them, "Why do you quarrel with me? Why do you test the Lord?" But the people thirsted there for water; and the people complained against Moses and said, "Why did you bring us out of Egypt, to kill us and our children and livestock with thirst?" So Moses cried out to the Lord, "What shall I do with this people? They are almost ready to stone me." The Lord said to Moses, "Go on ahead of the people, and take some of the elders of Israel with you; take in your hand the staff with which you struck the Nile, and go. I will be standing there in front of you on the rock at Horeb. Strike the rock, and water will come out of it, so that the people may drink." Moses did so, in the sight of the elders of Israel. He called the place Massah and Meribah, because the Israelites quarreled and tested the Lord, saying, "Is the Lord among us or not?"

Exodus 17: 2-7

## PRAYER

Lord, my God,
I stand in your presence today
keenly aware of the thirst in my soul,
those places that need your joy,
your hope, and your love.
Some days I feel so barren,
so tired and weary of the long journey
and of the struggles that life brings.
For all my striving to live in hope,
and my best intentions to walk in faith,
some days I'm just not up to it.
Lord, refresh my soul.
Rain down upon me
the living water of your grace.
Let this barren desert bloom again
with new life and beauty
so that I may help refresh others
who are tired and need hope.

## KEYSTONE

*"Come to the springs of grace."*

## SELF-REFLECTION

- What can I do this Lent to refresh my spirit?
- How can I become more mindful of God's gift of life?
- What can I do to bring refreshment to others?

# Turn
# to
# Me

*G*od will never stop loving us. But do we really believe, as St. Paul says, that nothing can separate us from the love of God? Consider those troubling secrets in your life that you've never shared, those things that cause you shame, the source of fear and insecurity. God knows them all and still loves us with no reservations, loving us more than we're able to love ourselves. Sometimes out of hurt and shame, or because we're afraid of what God might ask of us, or because we don't believe we're worthy, we turn our backs to run and hide from that love. We don't allow it to touch us and change our hearts. The invitation of Lent is that we turn to God and come home to the love that saves us and sets us free.

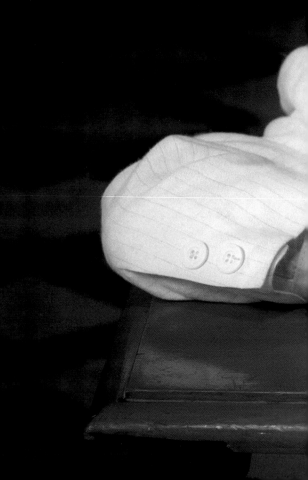

# Turn to Me

### SONG

**Turn to me, O turn and be saved,
says the Lord for I am God.
There is no other, none beside me.
I call your name.**

I am God who comforts you;
who are you to be afraid
of flesh that fades, is made like the grass of the field
soon to wither.

Listen to me, my people;
give ear to me, my nation:
a law will go forth from me, and my justice for a light
to the people.

Lift up your eyes to the heavens
and look at the earth down below.
The heavens will vanish like smoke
and the earth will wear out like a garment.

## SCRIPTURE

*Y*et even now, says the Lord, return to me with all your heart, with fasting, with weeping, and with mourning; rend your hearts and not your clothing. Return to the Lord, your God, for he is gracious and merciful, slow to anger, and abounding in steadfast love, and relents from punishing.

You shall eat in plenty and be satisfied, and praise the name of the Lord your God, who has dealt wondrously with you. And my people shall never again be put to shame. You shall know that I am in the midst of Israel, and that I, the Lord, am your God and there is no other. And my people shall never again be put to shame.

Joel 2:12-13, 26-27

## PRAYER

God of my heart,
I cannot completely fathom
how you could love me so completely.
There are no strings attached to your love.
I can't buy it or earn it,
and I certainly don't deserve it.
You love me and have created me in love.
At the same time you've given me
the power to refuse that love,
to hide from it, to run from it,
to set walls around my heart
that keep it from touching me.
I do this most often
because I'm afraid
of what your love may do to me,
of how it might change me,
of what it might require of me.
Lord, I turn to you and ask for the grace
to allow your love to touch my life.

## KEYSTONE

*"Return to me with all your heart."*

## SELF-REFLECTION

- What areas of my life need God's healing mercy?
- Am I willing to accept God's love and forgiveness?
- Who in my life might need a word of mercy from me?

# How Can I Repay

It's no surprise that God doesn't always answer our prayers the way we'd hope. At times we may struggle to trust that God is listening, but Christ teaches us that God always hears us when we pray with a sincere heart. In great and loving wisdom, God knows what we need better than we do and will provide for us exactly what we need. We may have to wait, but God knows when the time is right to bless us. Perhaps prayer is not so much a matter of convincing God to give us what we seek, but rather of opening our hearts to receive the gift God has prepared for us. When our hearts are humble, we come to recognize the great abundance of God's blessing.

## SONG

**How can I repay the kindness of the Lord?**
**What song can I sing to honor the name of God?**

When the darkness closes round me,
and I long to see your morning,
then you lean your face beside me
and whisper my name.

As I walk among the living,
I depend upon your kindness
to uphold my every footstep
and dry every tear.

As I stand before the people,
I will raise the cup of gladness,
and I vow to love and serve you
the rest of my days.

## SCRIPTURE

"*A*sk, and it will be given you; search, and you will find; knock, and the door will be opened for you. For everyone who asks receives, and everyone who searches finds, and for everyone who knocks, the door will be opened. Is there anyone among you who, if your child asks for bread, will give a stone? Or if the child asks for a fish, will give a snake? If you then, who are evil, know how to give good gifts to your children, how much more will your Father in heaven give good things to those who ask him!

"In everything do to others as you would have them do to you; for this is the law and the prophets."

Matthew 7:7-12

## PRAYER

God of great wisdom,
I've called your name many times
and wondered if you're listening.
I'm ashamed to say that sometimes
I don't yet trust your love for me.
Are you there? Are you listening?
Lord, teach me to be quiet and patient,
to wait for you in the silence of my prayer.
Help me to know in my heart
that you are closer to me than I am to myself.
Sometimes your timing is not what I'd want.
Sometimes the grace you have in store for me
is not the one I want to receive.
I'm not very patient, Lord,
but you already know that your work in me
is not yet complete.
Soften my heart, dear God.
Let me see your abundance all around me,
and let me never doubt your care for me.

## KEYSTONE

*"Ask and you shall receive."*

## SELF-REFLECTION

- Do I trust that God listens to my prayers?
- Do I share my heart with God or does my prayer lack conviction ?
- Do I make gratitude a priority in my life?

# From the Depths

*A*s the psalms of lamentation so poignantly express, we will all at one time or another raise our arms to heaven and cry, "Why, O Lord? Where have you gone? Have you forgotten me? How could you let this happen?" When the trials of life bring us to our knees, when we have the secure ground knocked out from under us, when there's no where else to go, we turn to the One in whom we place our hope. In that, our powerlessness becomes a grace, an opportunity to allow God to sustain us. As St. Paul suggests, our brokenness provides the opening for God's grace to enter into our hearts.

# From the Depths

### SONG

**O Lord, hear my prayer. From the depths, Lord, I call.**
**Do not turn from the sound of my pleading.**
**O God, be my hope. May your hand hold me fast**
**till I stand in the courts of your dwelling.**

If you should count our sin,
then who could hope for heaven?
But you, O Lord, are merciful;
forever is your love.

I wait in hope, O God,
to stand within your temple.
As watchmen wait for morning light,
my spirit longs for you.

## SCRIPTURE

*B*ut God, who is rich in mercy, out of the great love with which he loved us even when we were dead through our trespasses, made us alive together with Christ — by grace you have been saved — and raised us up with him and seated us with him in the heavenly places in Christ Jesus, so that in the ages to come he might show the immeasurable riches of his grace in kindness toward us in Christ Jesus. For by grace you have been saved through faith, and this is not your own doing; it is the gift of God — not the result of works, so that no one may boast. For we are what he has made us, created in Christ Jesus for good works, which God prepared beforehand to be our way of life.

Ephesians 2:4-9

## PRAYER

God, my help and my strength,
there are times when I find it so difficult
to continue living in hope.
I've had my heart broken,
known profound loss,
and had my dreams destroyed.
I've often failed in my attempts
to become the holy person
you created me to be.
And so I bring you all of this -
my failures, my disappointments,
my lost dreams and my broken heart -
and hope that you can make of it
something more, something better,
maybe even something holy.
Perhaps all these things
can be a way of hollowing out a place
in me to make more room in my soul
for you and for your redeeming love.
With all my heart, I hope it may be so.

## KEYSTONE

*"I wait in hope, O God."*

## SELF-REFLECTION

- Where do I feel most weak and vulnerable?
- Do I trust that God can turn my weakness into grace?
- Do I let Jesus be my companion in my darkest moments?

# Yahweh, the Faithful One

*F*aithfulness can only be measured over time and God proved his faithfulness to the people of Israel over many generations. By looking back on their story, they remembered all the ways that God had cared for them. Similarly, we can often only see how much God has watched over us when we look back on our lives to see what God has done. We may see how the path was not always smooth, but God was always there. We may carry the scars of heartaches and unfulfilled dreams, but the Lord has remained faithful to us through it all. And as he told Noah after the flood, every time we see a rainbow appearing after a storm, we should be reminded of that age-old Covenant. No matter what happens, God's love will last forever.

# Yahweh, the Faithful One

## SONG

**Yahweh's\* love will last forever,
his faithfulness till the end of time.
Yahweh is a loving God,
Yahweh the faithful one.**

Have no fear for I am with you.
I will be your shield.
Go now and leave your homeland
for I will give you a home.

You shall be my chosen people,
and I will be your God.
I will bless your name forever
and keep you from all harm.

\* Author's note: "Yahweh" is the translation of the name of God often found in the Jerusalem Bible, a literal translation of the Hebrew scripture commissioned by Pope Pius XII. This bible translation is approved by the Church for personal and communal prayer outside the celebration of liturgy.

## SCRIPTURE

"*T*herefore prophesy, and say to them, Thus says the Lord God: I am going to open your graves, and bring you up from your graves, O my people; and I will bring you back to the land of Israel. And you shall know that I am the Lord, when I open your graves, and bring you up from your graves, O my people. I will put my spirit within you, and you shall live, and I will place you on your own soil; then you shall know that I, the Lord, have spoken and will act, says the Lord.

They shall live in the land that I gave to my servant Jacob, in which your ancestors lived; they and their children and their children's children shall live there forever; and my servant David shall be their prince forever. I will make a covenant of peace with them; it shall be an everlasting covenant with them; and I will bless them and multiply them, and will set my sanctuary among them forevermore. My dwelling place shall be with them; and I will be their God, and they shall be my people. Then the nations shall know that I the Lord sanctify Israel, when my sanctuary is among them forevermore."

Ezecchiel 37:12-14, 25-28

## PRAYER

Lord, my God,
you remind us again and again
that your name is Faithful One
and God-With-Us.
In every age, in every place,
in every generation,
you've proven over and over
that you are true to your name.
The Covenant you made
so long ago with the people of Israel
stands as your promise to us all.
When I take the time
to look back on my life,
I can see your gracious love
providing for me, uplifting me,
protecting me, and summoning me forward.
Grant me, dear Lord,
the grace to be more mindful
of your faithful love sustaining me
always and everywhere.

## KEYSTONE

*"Have no fear for I am with you."*

## SELF-REFLECTION

- How do I daily remind myself of God's faithful love?
- Can I remember special moments where God was there for me?
- How might I be a sign of God's faithfulness to others?

# Hosanna to the Son of David

*T*he path of holiness for every human being summons great strength and courage. It involves becoming the unique person God created us to be. That's why learning to trust the special gifts, passions and events of our lives is so important and such a challenge. Was it just coincidence that brought Jesus to Jerusalem on this particular Passover or was it all part of the story waiting to be told? He is determined to follow the way of God no matter where that may lead. With a growing sense of foreboding, Jesus enters Jerusalem knowing the ever growing hatred of him by the Jewish leaders. After all, he was teaching people that the law of love must replace all the prescriptions of the Jewish law, the very foundation of Judaism. Jesus came to free us all with the message of God's love.

**SONG**

**Hosanna to the Son of David.**
**O blest is he, O blest is he**
**who comes in the name of the Lord.**

Rejoice, daughter of Zion,
in the one who brings great joy!
Sing praise, children of Judah,
for the Lord is close at hand!

Rejoice, all who are thirsting
for the streams of living joy!
Sing praise, children of Judah,
for the Lord is close at hand!

Rejoice, all who are longing
to behold the face of God!
Sing praise, children of Judah,
for the Lord is close at hand.

## SCRIPTURE

"Listen to me, O coastlands, pay attention, you peoples from far away! The Lord called me before I was born, while I was in my mother's womb he named me. He made my mouth like a sharp sword, in the shadow of his hand he hid me; he made me a polished arrow, in his quiver he hid me away. And he said to me, "You are my servant, Israel, in whom I will be glorified." But I said, "I have labored in vain, I have spent my strength for nothing and vanity; yet surely my cause is with the Lord, and my reward with my God."

And now the Lord says, who formed me in the womb to be his servant, to bring Jacob back to him, and that Israel might be gathered to him, for I am honored in the sight of the Lord, and my God has become my strength — he says, "It is too light a thing that you should be my servant to raise up the tribes of Jacob and to restore the survivors of Israel; I will give you as a light to the nations, that my salvation may reach to the end of the earth."

Isaiah 49:1-6

## PRAYER

God, my hope and my strength,
grant me the courage
to walk into an unknown future.
None of us are exempt from the realities of life,
from suffering and loneliness.
I'm afraid of death and the loss of those I hold dear.
I'd rather not have to walk through that
and wish it could be different.
But I've chosen to walk with your son Jesus,
who embraced darkness and death
so that they might be redeemed,
so that they might be more than defeat.
I wish there was another way, Lord
but I will try my best to walk the way of Jesus,
and to trust that you are there with me
and will never forsake me,
especially in the darkest of times.
Even when I'm overwhelmed by fear,
grant me the grace to trust that your love
will in the end bring eternal joy.

## KEYSTONE

*"The Lord is close at hand."*

## SELF-REFLECTION

- What are the special gifts I bring to God's people?
- Can I step beyond the fear that sometimes grips my heart?
- How can I better strive to become the person God created
  me to be?

48

# Only This I Want

On the path of faith, the one thing from which all else flows is our relationship with God and with Christ through the indwelling of God's Spirit. When we allow it to mature, the power of this relationship is reflected in our words and deeds. As St. Augustine suggests, "To fall in love with God is the greatest romance." Just as we come to know those we love by spending time with them, so too we come to recognize the movements of God's Spirit in our lives by growing in intimacy with the God of our heart. Love takes work. We can't really know God unless we're willing to spend time as friends do - quiet time, talking, listening, laughing, crying and cherishing each other's company.

## SONG

**Only this I want: but to know the Lord,**
**and to bear his cross so to wear the crown he wore.**

All but this is loss, worthless refuse to me,
for to gain the Lord is to gain all I need.

I will run the race; I will fight the good fight,
so to win the prize of the kingdom of my Lord.

Let your heart be glad, always glad in the Lord,
so to shine like stars in the darkness of the night.

## SCRIPTURE

*N*ow among those who went up to worship at the festival were some Greeks. They came to Philip, who was from Bethsaida in Galilee, and said to him, "Sir, we wish to see Jesus." Philip went and told Andrew; then Andrew and Philip went and told Jesus. Jesus answered them, "The hour has come for the Son of Man to be glorified. Very truly, I tell you, unless a grain of wheat falls into the earth and dies, it remains just a single grain; but if it dies, it bears much fruit. Those who love their life lose it, and those who hate their life in this world will keep it for eternal life."

Jesus said to them, "The light is with you for a little longer. Walk while you have the light, so that the darkness may not overtake you. If you walk in the darkness, you do not know where you are going. While you have the light, believe in the light, so that you may become children of light."

John 12:20-25, 35-36

## PRAYER

O God, my teacher and Lord,
I come humbly before you
with a simple request:
help me to know your heart.
Be patient with me
as I try to understand
the wisdom of your ways
and the truth of your love.
I hope that in coming to know you
my heart will become
more like yours,
that I will learn to love
a little more like you love.
Perhaps the day will arrive
when I come to know you well enough
that I forget for a moment
that you are my God
and will dare to call you my friend.

## KEYSTONE

*"I would like to see Jesus."*

## SELF-REFLECTION

- Do I truly desire to know God?
- Do I believe that God wants to share his heart with me?
- Am I afraid to know God because of where it might lead?

# As I Have Done for You

*T*his day takes us to the heart of our Christian faith. This is a feast of companionship, of hospitality, of love. It's been said that Jesus of Nazareth was not put to death because of what he taught but because of who he ate with - the outcasts, the poor, the sick, the oppressed, the sinner. This day should stir within us a reminder of how far we fall short of loving the way our Lord and Teacher loves us. "Love one another as I have loved you," was his great commission to his followers. And then, as if he knew we wouldn't understand, he shows us by getting down on his hands and knees to wash the dirt off our feet. We are so privileged to be among those he considers his friends.

# As I Have Done for You

### SONG

**I, your Lord and Master, now become your servant.**
**I, who made the moon and stars, will kneel to wash your feet.**
**This is my commandment: to love as I have loved you.**
**Kneel to wash each other's feet as I have done for you.**

All the world will know you are my disciples
by the love that you offer, the kindness you show.
You have heard the voice of God in the words that I have spoken.
You beheld heaven's glory and have seen the face of God.

I must leave you now only for a moment.
I must go to my Father to make you a home.
On the day of my return I will come to take you with me
to the place I have promised where your joy will have no end.

## SCRIPTURE

*A*nd during supper, Jesus, knowing that the Father had given all things into his hands, and that he had come from God and was going to God, got up from the table, took off his outer robe, and tied a towel around himself. Then he poured water into a basin and began to wash the disciples' feet and to wipe them with the towel that was tied around him.

After he had washed their feet, had put on his robe, and had returned to the table, he said to them, "Do you know what I have done to you? You call me Teacher and Lord — and you are right, for that is what I am. So if I, your Lord and Teacher, have washed your feet, you also ought to wash one another's feet. For I have set you an example, that you also should do as I have done to you. Very truly, I tell you, servants are not greater than their master, nor are messengers greater than the one who sent them. If you know these things, you are blessed if you do them.

John 13:3-5,12-17

## PRAYER

Most mysterious God,
just when I think
I understand what you ask of me,
I find out that I've been wrong all along.
It's a bit hard for me to fathom
how the same One who is my Lord and God
would get down on his knees to wash my feet.
You know my feet aren't very pretty;
they've traveled a long way
and show many signs of wear.
They're dirty from the journey
and I wish they were more presentable.
But I watch with my heart in my throat
as you gently take my feet
and wash them ever so carefully.
And then, if that wasn't enough,
you bend low to kiss them with a smile.

## KEYSTONE

*"You should do as I have done."*

## SELF-REFLECTION

- How might I foster in myself the heart of a servant?
- Am I willing to embrace with love those who are different from me?
- Do I pray for my enemies and those who have hurt me?

---

# Be My Refuge

---

*O*f only there could be another way of accomplishing the purpose of our lives. But there's no getting around it. Death must have its way with each of us. From ashes to ashes and dust unto dust. God doesn't promise us a way out, an escape from the destiny that lies ahead for every creature. But God does promise to stand with us, both in life and in death, just as he stood with his own beloved Son who embraced a shameful death on a cross. The prophet Jeremiah even suggests a God who weeps as a parent would mourn at the death of their child. If the most frightening thing about death is the veil that hides what's on the other side, the death of Jesus tore that veil and removed it forever. Christ has revealed to hearts of faith that death is but a threshold into the Kingdom of God.

# Be My Refuge

**SONG**

**Father, be my refuge.**
**Into your hands I commend my spirit.**

O God, my God, be my refuge and strength.
Be true to your promise and keep me from harm.
Though my foes all laugh when I call out your name,
I will count on your mercy and cling to your love.

My eyes now burn with the salt of my tears.
My soul has been broken, my body is torn.
May your love rise up to encircle my life,
like a strong mighty fortress to shelter and shield.

To you, O God, I surrender my life.
I place in your bosom the dreams of my heart.
All my friends have fled and have left me alone,
yet I know you are faithful, my rock and my hope.

## SCRIPTURE

So they took Jesus; and carrying the cross by himself, he went out to what is called The Place of the Skull, which in Hebrew is called Golgotha. There they crucified him, and with him two others, one on either side, with Jesus between them. Pilate also had an inscription written and put on the cross. It read, "Jesus of Nazareth, the King of the Jews."

Meanwhile, standing near the cross of Jesus were his mother, and his mother's sister, Mary the wife of Clopas, and Mary Magdalene. When Jesus saw his mother and the disciple whom he loved standing beside her, he said to his mother, "Woman, here is your son." Then he said to the disciple, "Here is your mother." And from that hour the disciple took her into his own home.

A jar full of sour wine was standing there. So they put a sponge full of the wine on a branch of hyssop and held it to his mouth. When Jesus had received the wine, he said, "It is finished." Then he bowed his head and gave up his spirit.

John 19:17-19,25-26,29-30

## PRAYER

God, my hope,
I don't know what to do
or to whom to turn.
I feel so utterly helpless
and stretched to the limits
of my humanity.
I never imagined that I'd ever experience
such a complete sense of powerlessness.
Lord, my faithful friend,
I place myself and my life
and my destiny in your hands.
With my weak and fragile faith,
grant me the grace to trust your love
to bring me out of this darkness.
Even in the mystery of my mortality
and the emptiness of this dark night,
I give my life to you
to do with it what your love
would bring to birth.

## KEYSTONE

*"Father, be my refuge."*

## SELF-REFLECTION

- When and where has my heart been broken?
- How do I deal with loneliness on my journey?
- How has God been a refuge for me?

# Holy Darkness

Imagine what it might have been like as the friends and family of Jesus huddled together on that first Holy Saturday. Jesus was gone. They'd watched him die an excruciatingly painful and shameful death. Mary, Peter, John, Mary Magdalene and all the others hardly able to grasp what had happened, and much less able to know what to do next. They surely would have tried as best they could to comfort each other. But when one's own sorrow is so profound, that's hard to do. The one they'd loved as a son, a friend and teacher, was gone. It would be hard to imagine that even God could have a purpose to it all.

## SONG

**Holy darkness, blessed night,**
**heaven's answer hidden from our sight.**
**As we await you, O God of silence,**
**we embrace your holy night.**

I have tried you in fires of affliction.
I have taught your soul to grieve.
In the barren soil of your loneliness,
there I will plant my seed.

I have taught you the price of compassion;
you have stood before the grave.
Though my love can seem like a raging storm,
this is the love that saves.

In your deepest hour of darkness,
I will give you wealth untold.
When the silence stills your spirit,
will my riches fill your soul.

## SCRIPTURE

*W*hen it was evening, there came a rich man from Arimathea, named Joseph, who was also a disciple of Jesus. He went to Pilate and asked for the body of Jesus; then Pilate ordered it to be given to him. So Joseph took the body and wrapped it in a clean linen cloth and laid it in his own new tomb, which he had hewn in the rock. He then rolled a great stone to the door of the tomb and went away.

Mary Magdalene and the other Mary were there, sitting opposite the tomb. The next day, that is, after the day of Preparation, the chief priests and the Pharisees gathered before Pilate and said, "Sir, we remember what that impostor said while he was still alive, 'After three days I will rise again.' Therefore command the tomb to be made secure until the third day; otherwise his disciples may go and steal him away, and tell the people, 'He has been raised from the dead,' and the last deception would be worse than the first."

Matthew 19:57-64

71

## PRAYER

God of my heart,
I've experienced loss before
but nothing as profound as this.
It's as though someone took my heart
and tore it so completely that I don't know
if I'll ever again feel joy and peace.
I imagine Jesus, my friend and brother,
the one in whom I place my hope,
lying dead in my arms.
How could this possibly
be part of your eternal plan?
All I can do is weep and feel the hopelessness.
The temptation to despair seems very real.
Let me find comfort
in my brothers and sisters.
Let me do my best to comfort them in return.
May there be something
in our brokenness that provides an opening
for you to touch our darkness and make it holy.

## KEYSTONE

*"We embrace your holy night."*

## SELF-REFLECTION

- How do I respond to another person's suffering?
- Can I forget myself and set aside my own hurt to reach out and comfort others?
- How might I help to heal my own grief and losses?

# Join in the Dance

Nothing is impossible with God. On this holy day of Easter something happened that no one ever thought possible. Death, the very thing that can overwhelm us with sorrow, has itself been robbed forever of its power. Today death itself has died. We no longer need be afraid because it has been revealed today that God's love is stronger than death. No matter the darkness through which we must pass, no matter the heartache we must endure, love will always win. While most of us do much better living with sadness, today is a day to open hearts to drink deeply of God's divine joy that his Son, and all his children, will never again be defeated by death. Let us today imagine a God, like the God in Zephaniah 3:17, who rejoices over us with glad song and dances with shouts of joy for us.

# Join in the Dance

### SONG

**Join in the dance of the earth's jubilation!**
**This is the feast of the love of God.**
**Shout from the heights to the ends of creation:**
**Jesus, the Savior, is risen from the grave!**

Wake, O people, sleep no longer,
greet the breaking day.
Christ, Redeemer, Lamb and Lion,
turns the night away!

All creation, like a mother,
labors to give birth.
Soon the pain will be forgotten,
joy for all the earth!

Now our shame becomes our glory
on this holy tree.
Now the reign of death is ended;
now we are set free!

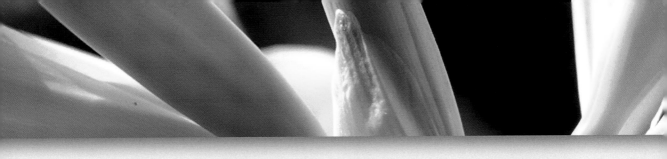

## SCRIPTURE

*B*ut on the first day of the week, at early dawn, they came to the tomb, taking the spices that they had prepared. They found the stone rolled away from the tomb, but when they went in, they did not find the body. While they were perplexed about this, suddenly two men in dazzling clothes stood beside them. The women were terrified and bowed their faces to the ground, but the men said to them, "Why do you look for the living among the dead? He is not here, but has risen. Remember how he told you, while he was still in Galilee, that the Son of Man must be handed over to sinners, and be crucified, and on the third day rise again." Then they remembered his words, and returning from the tomb, they told all this to the eleven and to all the rest.

But these words seemed to them an idle tale, and they did not believe them. But Peter got up and ran to the tomb; stooping and looking in, he saw the linen cloths by themselves; then he went home, amazed at what had happened.

Luke 24:1-9, 11-12

## PRAYER

God of endless surprises,
I could never begin to imagine
that this would be how the story would end.
Yesterday felt so final.
I would never have guessed
that you had yet to play your wildcard,
the one that turns the end into the beginning,
the one that dares to laugh in the face of death
because you know that death will never be the end.
Thank you, dearest God,
for your love
that will always and forever
be stronger than death.
Today, grant that I may share your joy,
that I may know just a small measure
of the happiness that is yours
when your Son woke from the sleep of death.
Let your joy enter into those deepest places of my soul
that so need to know and believe.

## KEYSTONE

*"Let me know great joy."*

## SELF-REFLECTION

- Where do I experience the new life that's all around us?
- Can I share the joy of another as if it's my own?
- Do I allow myself to drink deeply of God's joy at Easter?

# Our Hope is in the Lord

Love always wins. That's the message of Easter. No matter how awful things seem to be, no matter how bleak and hopeless, the resurrection of Christ reassures us that in the end new life will come from death. Just when we feel that the darkness will overwhelm us, and hope seems futile, we hear the Savior quietly speak our name, just as he spoke Mary Magdalene's as she mourned outside the tomb. In our heart of faith we know it is the voice of our beloved Christ, the Risen Lord. Something deep in our being knows this voice because it's the same one that spoke our name from the beginning of time, the same voice we heard singing a love song we were born and were placed in our parents arms. God knows each of us by name.

# Our Hope is in the Lord

### SONG

Our hope is in the Lord, who neither sleeps nor slumbers,
who stands with us by light of day and guards us through the night.
While kingdoms rise and fall, the love of God stands firm.
Though mountains quake and crumble, God's promise shall endure.

Our lives are like the grass that quickly fades and withers.
Our days are like a grain of sand upon the ocean floor.
While kingdoms rise and fall, the love of God stands firm.
Though mountains quake and crumble, God's promise shall endure.

So far beyond our sight the ways of God our Maker.
So hard for us to understand the wisdom of the Lord.
While kingdoms rise and fall, the love of God stands firm.
Though mountains quake and crumble, God's promise shall endure.

## SCRIPTURE

*B*ut Mary stood weeping outside the tomb. As she wept, she bent over to look into the tomb; and she saw two angels in white, sitting where the body of Jesus had been lying, one at the head and the other at the feet. They said to her, "Woman, why are you weeping?" She said to them, "They have taken away my Lord, and I do not know where they have laid him."

When she had said this, she turned around and saw Jesus standing there, but she did not know that it was Jesus. Jesus said to her, "Woman, why are you weeping? Whom are you looking for?" Supposing him to be the gardener, she said to him, "Sir, if you have carried him away, tell me where you have laid him, and I will take him away." Jesus said to her, "Mary!" She turned and said to him in Hebrew, "Rabbouni!" (which means Teacher).

Jesus said to her, "Go to my brothers and say to them, 'I am ascending to my Father and your Father, to my God and your God.'"

John 20:11-17

## PRAYER

God of beauty and splendor,
I'm sure there are times when you smile,
and perhaps even laugh at me.
I can imagine that you
take delight as you watch me
look for hope and life
in all the wrong places.
All the most marvelous creatures of this world,
the people and things that are so beautiful,
are but a shadow of the beauty
and goodness that is yours.
Lord, grant me the grace
to see this world with all its beauty
as your gift to be used
insofar as it brings me closer to you,
my Creator and Lord.
May I come to find in everything
a glimpse of your goodness and beauty.

## KEYSTONE

*"Love always wins."*

## SELF-REFLECTION

- Where do I find hope?
- Can I wait for God's promise to be fulfilled?
- How might I be a source of light and hope to others?

# Only
# in
# God

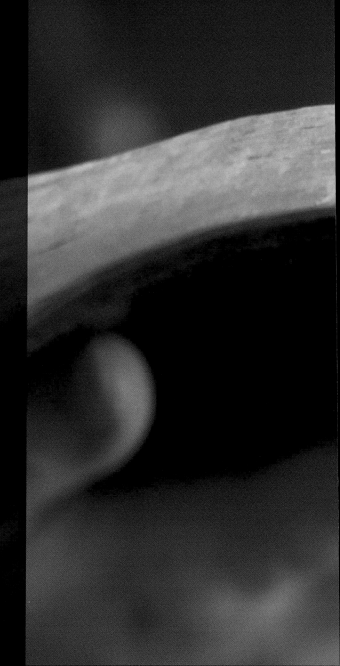

*E*very one of us longs for peace, for a place of security where we can live and grow and prosper. After the events of Good Friday, the disciples and friends of Jesus were so afraid, terrified that those who killed Jesus would now come seeking them, and worried about a future with so many unanswered questions. It's significant that "Peace!" is the Risen Christ's first greeting to his friends. He offers them reassurance that everything will be alright in the end. So too, we must not allow fear to keep us frozen. Instead, must begin to trust the prompting of the Spirit of Christ to show us how to proceed and hold onto the reassurance that the Risen Lord is always with us. We will recognize his presence by the peace he speaks to our hearts.

## SONG

**Only in God will my soul be at rest;**
**from him comes my hope my salvation.**
**He alone is my rock of safety, my strength,**
**my glory, my God.**

Trust in him at all times, O people,
and pour out your hearts.
God Himself is a refuge for us
and a stronghold for our fear.

Many times have I heard him tell
of His long lasting love.
You Yourself, Lord, reward all who labor
for love of your name.

## SCRIPTURE

*W*hen it was evening on that day, the first day of the week, and the doors of the house where the disciples had met were locked for fear of the Jews, Jesus came and stood among them and said, "Peace be with you." After he said this, he showed them his hands and his side. Then the disciples rejoiced when they saw the Lord. Jesus said to them again, "Peace be with you. As the Father has sent me, so I send you."

But Thomas, one of the twelve, was not with them when Jesus came. So the other disciples told him, "We have seen the Lord." But he said to them, "Unless I see the mark of the nails in his hands, and put my finger in the mark of the nails and my hand in his side, I will not believe."

A week later his disciples were again in the house, and Thomas was with them. Then he said to Thomas, "Put your finger here and see my hands. Reach out your hand and put it in my side. Do not doubt but believe." Thomas answered him, "My Lord and my God!"

John 20:19-21, 24-28

## PRAYER

Lord, my God,
sometimes all I want Is for the race to stop
so that I can rest for a bit.
I have to admit that I don't do very well
at taking care of this body
you've entrusted to me.
I often treat it with such disrespect
that I'm surprised it just doesn't stop.
Sometimes it lets me know
that it just can't go an farther
without a break and without nourishment.
This is even more true for my spirit,
which I fail to attend to as well.
Lord, grant me the grace
to know when I need to rest.
Let me be consoled
by simply resting in your presence
and allowing you to renew me
both in body and in spirit.

## KEYSTONE

*"Peace be with you."*

## SELF-REFLECTION

- What people or situations cause me turmoil?
- Do I help Christ's peace to flourish around me?
- When and where do I experience the peace that Christ promised?

# Come, Stay with Us

*W*hy do we not recognize him? Why do we travel so long without knowing his voice and feeling his hand on our shoulder? Two of Jesus' close companions walk most of the day in his presence and still their eyes do not see. They're so much like us. At every turn we miss his voice, his touch, the movement of his Spirit in our hearts. It's often only when we take time to look back that we realize that our hearts were "burning within us" as we heard words that spoke of love, mercy, kindness, hope and consolation. This is exactly what we are invited to do at Eucharist: to remember and give thanks. When we tell the stories and share the bread and cup we became what we eat, the Body of Christ.

# Come, Stay with Us

### SONG

Come, stay with us, O Lord, for the day is nearly ended.
We have journeyed far since morning and we long for peaceful rest.

**As evening closes 'round us, may you speak to us of heaven,
as you fill the night with stars, O Lord, and sing the world to sleep.**

Come, stay with us, O Lord, as we tell the wondrous stories
of a cave with kings and shepherds, and the day a blind man saw.

Come, stay with us, O Lord, as we wait in fear and sadness
for the One we've loved and longed for is asleep among the dead.

Come, stay with us, O Lord, that our hearts may burn within us
as we come to know and love you in the breaking of the bread.

## SCRIPTURE

*N*ow on that same day two of them were going to a village called Emmaus, about seven miles from Jerusalem, and talking with each other about all these things that had happened. While they were talking and discussing, Jesus himself came near and went with them, but their eyes were kept from recognizing him.

As they came near the village to which they were going, he walked ahead as if he were going on. But they urged him strongly, saying, "Stay with us, because it is almost evening and the day is now nearly over." So he went in to stay with them. When he was at the table with them, he took bread, blessed and broke it, and gave it to them. Then their eyes were opened, and they recognized him; and he vanished from their sight. They said to each other, "Were not our hearts burning within us while he was talking to us on the road, while he was opening the scriptures to us?"

Luke 24:13-14, 28-32

## PRAYER

Lord and Savior,
you showed yourself always ready
to welcome anyone and everyone
into the circle of your friendship.
It didn't matter if they were saints or sinners,
friends or strangers, from wealth or from poverty.
There was a place for everyone
because you saw them all as God sees them.
At least I know that there's a place
for me at the table too.
Grant me the grace, dear Lord,
to grow a heart as large as yours
welcoming everyone, especially the unlovely,
those who are alone and those who are left out.
And most especially, Lord,
let me welcome you into my life,
to be my companion
and my friend.
Come, stay with me, Lord.

## KEYSTONE

*"Come, stay with me, Lord."*

## SELF-REFLECTION

- Do I allow Jesus to be my companion through life?
- When have I experienced the Spirit of Jesus teaching me about the Scriptures?
- Where is my passion? What inspires me?

# Simon, Son of John

I t's been suggested that we make ourselves profoundly vulnerable when we ask someone the question, "Do you love me?" The other person is rarely so forthright as to just say "no." More often, there's just a non-committal answer, a change of subject, or a slow, subtle pulling away from time spent together. But the message is still clear. It's even more fearsome when we ask the question of a dear friend, and perhaps one who's broken our heart. And then when someone we love dearly responds without hesitation, "Yes, of course I love you", it fills us with great comfort and joy. St. Ignatius of Loyola speaks with wisdom when he suggests that love shows itself more clearly in deeds than in words. Of course, the words are important, but our works of love truly reveal the depth of our love.

## SONG

**Simon, son of John, do you love me?**
**Will you take my cross? Will you follow me?**
**Do you love me more than these?**

Though teacher and Lord, I call you my friend,
no longer my servant. Who do you say that I am?

If you are my friend, then care for my sheep.
If you would go with me, stand as the rock that can weep.

Remember the day you stood on this shore
with nets nearly bursting, filled with the bounty of God.

## SCRIPTURE

*W*hen they had finished breakfast, Jesus said to Simon Peter, "Simon son of John, do you love me more than these?" He said to him, "Yes, Lord; you know that I love you." Jesus said to him, "Feed my lambs."

A second time he said to him, "Simon son of John, do you love me?" He said to him, "Yes, Lord; you know that I love you." Jesus said to him, "Tend my sheep."

He said to him the third time, "Simon son of John, do you love me?" Peter felt hurt because he said to him the third time, "Do you love me?" And he said to him, "Lord, you know everything; you know that I love you." Jesus said to him, "Feed my sheep. Very truly, I tell you, when you were younger, you used to fasten your own belt and to go wherever you wished. But when you grow old, you will stretch out your hands, and someone else will fasten a belt around you and take you where you do not wish to go."

John 21:15-18

## PRAYER

Dearest, Lord,
you know that I love you.
Your love and companionship
mean more to me than anything.
Grant me the grace to understand
that you hope that I will return that love.
Because love shows itself more perfectly
in deeds rather than just words,
I hope I can live in such a way
that I will show my love for you
by loving those who are dear to your heart.
They may not always be the ones
I'd choose to love,
but they are the ones
you send into my life for a reason.
Perhaps I can add
just a bit more joy to their lives
and help them to understand
how beloved they are in your eyes.

## KEYSTONE

*"Do you love me?"*

## SELF-REFLECTION

· How do I respond when Jesus asks me, "Do you love me?
· Have I ever felt betrayed by a friend or loved one? Am I able to forgive them?
· Today, at this moment, where is Jesus asking me to follow?

# All for Your Glory

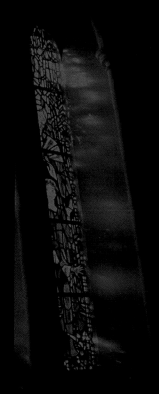

*A*s is so evident in the stories of those first disciples who experienced the Risen Lord, it took time for them to assimilate what had happened and to understand what it meant. And after the Ascension, they surely wrestled with how Jesus, the Risen One, continued to be present among them. The Spirit of the Risen Lord continued to abide with them, giving both them and us a new way to see this world. Christ was present beyond the confinements of physical flesh and bone, and now could be found and experienced at the center of all reality. All that is, was, and every will be is permeated with the presence of Christ who draws all things to himself. And one day, in the fullness of time, Christ will bring all things to the greater glory of God.

## SONG

Christ in our waking, Christ in our sleep,
Christ in the treasure of mem'ries we keep.
All the day's laughter, all the day's tears,
it is all for your glory, my Lord and my God.

Christ in our labor, Christ in our rest,
Christ in the faces of pilgrim and guest.
All of life's wonder, all of life's woe,
it is all for your glory, my Lord and my God.

Christ in the thunder, Christ in the calm,
Christ in the healing of music's sweet balm.
All of life's silence, all of life's song,
it is all for your glory, my Lord and my God.

Christ at our starting, Christ at our end,
Christ in our longing for journeys to end.
All that we've treasured, all that we've lost,
it is all for your glory, my Lord and my God.

## SCRIPTURE

*I* consider that the sufferings of this present time are not worth comparing with the glory about to be revealed to us. For the creation waits with eager longing for the revealing of the children of God; for the creation was subjected to futility, not of its own will but by the will of the one who subjected it, in hope that the creation itself will be set free from its bondage to decay and will obtain the freedom of the glory of the children of God. We know that the whole creation has been groaning in labor pains until now; and not only the creation, but we ourselves, who have the first fruits of the Spirit, groan inwardly while we wait for adoption, the redemption of our bodies. For in hope we were saved. Now hope that is seen is not hope. For who hopes for what is seen? But if we hope for what we do not see, we wait for it with patience. Likewise the Spirit helps us in our weakness; for we do not know how to pray as we ought, but that very Spirit intercedes with sighs too deep for words.

Romans 8:18-26

## PRAYER

Lord of all things,
I come before you
asking for a special favor.
Please grant me the grace
to see beneath the surface of things,
to begin to understand
that you are at the heart of everything.
Give me sight
to see your eyes looking at me
in the faces of those I meet.
Let me approach all the activities
of my day as opportunities
to offer you my thanks
and to give you glory.
In all things, Lord,
help me always choose what will be
for your greater honor and glory.

## KEYSTONE

*"All for your glory, O God."*

## SELF-REFLECTION

- How might I foster in myself a sense of Christ at the heart of everything?
- Where do I experience the Risen Lord in my life?
- How would my life change if Jesus appeared to me?

# So the Lord is to Me

*T*he disciples of Jesus, those who'd known him as friend and companion, wanted to share their joy with others. They wanted others to know him too. But how does one put into words the experience of Christ that had changed their lives? Our human language seems so inadequate and can never truly convey what we mean. And it's even more difficult when we try to describe a person we've come to love. How do we tell someone what Christ means to us? In the end, when we try to share our experience of God with others, we need to trust that the Spirit will give us the right words and will be at work in the hearts of those who listen to us. But the most powerful message we speak is the way we live. As Tertullian wrote of those early Christians, "See how they love one another."

## SONG

As the bridegroom to the chosen, as the shepherd to the sheep,
as the watchman to the city, so the Lord is to me.
As the fountain to the garden, as the fragrance to the rose,
as the sweetness to the honey, so the Lord is to me.

**My Light, my Way, my Truth, my Joy,
my God and my Savior. Christ all in all to me.**

As the master to the servant, as the mason to the stone,
as the singer to the music, so the Lord is to me.
As the father to the orphan, as the mother to the child,
as the lover to be loved, so the Lord is to me.

As the author to the story, as the potter to the clay,
as the healer to the broken, so the Lord is to me.
As the springtime to the winter, as the rainbow to the storm,
as the sunrise to the darkness, so the Lord is to me.

## SCRIPTURE

*B*eloved, let us love one another, because love is from God; everyone who loves is born of God and knows God. Whoever does not love does not know God, for God is love. God's love was revealed among us in this way: God sent his only Son into the world so that we might live through him. In this is love, not that we loved God but that he loved us and sent his Son to be the atoning sacrifice for our sins.

Beloved, since God loved us so much, we also ought to love one another. No one has ever seen God; if we love one another, God lives in us, and his love is perfected in us. By this we know that we abide in him and he in us, because he has given us of his Spirit.

God abides in those who confess that Jesus is the Son of God, and they abide in God. So we have known and believe the love that God has for us. God is love, and those who abide in love abide in God, and God abides in them.

1 John 4:7-13,15-16

## PRAYER

God of my heart,
there's so much I've yet to learn
about you and your ways.
You mean more to me
than anyone and anything.
Sometimes my heart
overflows with a sense
of wonder as I gaze upon your world
and watch how you care for your children.
Lord, grant me the grace
to stand in awe of your goodness,
to marvel at your kindness
and to allow you to enter
ever more completely
into my life and my heart.
Be my everything
and fill me, my God,
with joy and hope.

## KEYSTONE

*"Christ, all in all to me."*

## SELF-REFLECTION

- What images of God are most dear to my heart?
- Do I experience the joy of my relationship with God?
- How might I share this joy with others?

# Litany of the Holy Spirit

What exactly happened to the disciples on that first Pentecost? It must have been something profound enough that they no longer felt it necessary to lock themselves away in fear. It must have been something that gave them the courage to proclaim boldly that Jesus of Nazareth was alive, that he'd appeared to them and commissioned them to bear the good news of his message to the ends of the earth. They'd come to recognize the presence of the Risen Lord wherever they saw the fruits of the Spirit: charity, joy, peace, patience, kindness, goodness, gentleness faithfulness and generosity. And the people to whom they spoke saw the Spirit of Jesus in their eyes, on their faces, in their hearts and in the way they treated others.

## SONG

Come, O Holy Spirit, renew the face of the earth.
Come, O Bringer of Blessing, renew the face of the earth.
Come, O Font of Knowledge, renew the face of the earth.
Come, O Promise of Plenty, renew the face of the earth.

Come, O Word of Kindness, renew the face of the earth.
Come, O Mother of Mercy, renew the face of the earth.
Come, O Light of Wisdom, renew the face of the earth.
Come, O Giver of Gladness, renew the face of the earth.

Hope of all who hunger, renew the face of the earth.
Teacher of Truth and Justice, renew the face of the earth.
Breath of life eternal, renew the face of the earth.
Fullness of God within us, renew the face of the earth.

Song of joy and gladness, renew the face of the earth.
Author of Love's great story, renew the face of the earth.
Come, O Holy Spirit, renew the face of the earth.
Kindle your fire within us, renew the face of the earth.

## SCRIPTURE

*O*f the Spirit of him who raised Jesus from the dead dwells in you, he who raised Christ from the dead will give life to your mortal bodies also through his Spirit that dwells in you.

So then, brothers and sisters, we are debtors, not to the flesh, to live according to the flesh - for if you live according to the flesh, you will die; but if by the Spirit you put to death the deeds of the body, you will live. For all who are led by the Spirit of God are children of God. For you did not receive a spirit of slavery to fall back into fear, but you have received a spirit of adoption. When we cry, "Abba! Father!" it is that very Spirit bearing witness with our spirit that we are children of God, and if children, then heirs, heirs of God and joint heirs with Christ - if, in fact, we suffer with him so that we may also be glorified with him.

Romans 8:11-17

## PRAYER

Spirit of God,
may your wondrous fire
descend upon me
and kindle in my heart
a new passion to follow Jesus.
Grant me a new courage
that allows the good news
of his rising from death
to become evident in the way I live.
Renew my determination, blessed Spirit,
so that people may recognize in me
a new fire, a new hope,
a new strengh of loving.
Give me the wisdom and insight
to be able to discern your movement
within me and around me.
And above all, Holy Spirit,
let me trust that you
hold all things in your care.

## KEYSTONE

*"Kindle in me the fire of your love."*

## SELF-REFLECTION

- Where do I see evidence of the gifts of the Spirit?
- Do I really trust that the Spirit is guiding the Church?
- How might I foster in myself a renewed sense of the Spirit moving in my life?

# RESOURCES

The individual songs included on the compact disc, along with all of Dan Schutte's music, can also be found in the iTunes store.

The following are the songs featured in this book:

| | |
|---|---|
| *Ashes to Ashes* | *Dan Schutte* |
| *Let All Who Thirst* | *Dan Schutte* |
| *Turn to Me* | *John Foley, S.J.* |
| *How Can I Repay* | *Dan Schutte* |
| *From the Depths* | *Dan Schutte* |
| *Yahweh, the Faithful One* | *Dan Schutte* |
| *Hosanna to the Son of David* | *Dan Schutte* |
| *Only This I Want* | *Dan Schutte* |
| *As I Have Done For You* | *Dan Schutte* |
| *Be My Refuge* | *Dan Schutte* |
| *Holy Darkness* | *Dan Schutte* |
| *Join in the Dance* | *Dan Schutte* |
| *Our Hope Is In The Lord* | *Dan Schutte* |
| *Only in God* | *John Foley, S.J.* |
| *Come, Stay With Us* | *Dan Schutte)* |
| *Simon, Son of John* | *Dan Schutte* |
| *Valleys of Green* | *Dan Schutte* |
| *So the Lord Is To Me* | *Dan Schutte* |
| *Litany of the Holy Spirit* | *Dan Schutte* |

The digital edition of this prayer book can be found on the iBook Store. It requires the free iBook Reader app and is designed for optimal viewing on the iPad. The music tracks are embedded in the iBook edition which allows them to be played directly from the lyric page without an internet connection.

Visit Dan Schutte Music at *www.danschuttemusic.com* for more of Dan's music, including his book *Walking the Sacred Path: Spiritual Exercises for Today*. For music scores, music books and his complete music catalog, visit *www.ocp*.org.

For more information about Dan Schutte, his music, books and art, visit his website at *www.danschutte.com*.

CREDITS

**Book Layout & Design:** Dan Schutte

**Project Management:** Debbie McAuliffe

**Consulting Editor:** Fran Endicott Armstrong

**Concept Development:** Mike Gale

**Audio Re-Mastering:** Dan Schutte

**First iBooks Edition:** January 2015

**Print Edition:** *www.PilgrimMusic.com*

Very special thanks to John Foley, S.J. for the use of his two beautiful songs, "Turn to Me" and "Only in God," and to Jerry Chiusano for his magnificent piano renditions of them.

# FROM
# ASHES
# TO GLORY

A Prayer Book for Lent & Easter

## DAN SCHUTTE

# FROM
# ASHES
# TO GLORY

"*W*e should glory in the cross of our Lord Jesus Christ, for He is our salvation, our life and our resurrection; through Him we are saved and set free."

Entrance Antiphon for the Liturgy of Holy Thursday